Decorative
Mosaics

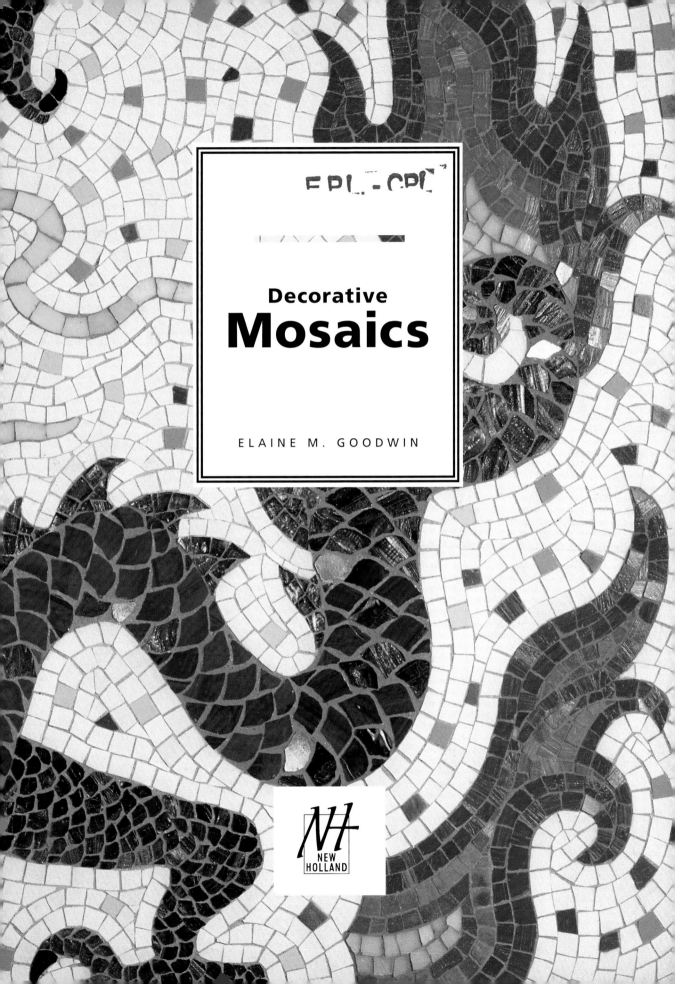

Decorative
Mosaics

ELAINE M. GOODWIN

NH
NEW
HOLLAND

"The mosaic surface from broken fragments
reflects a beauteous smile."
E.M.G.

This edition first published in 2005 by
New Holland Publishers Ltd
London • Cape Town • Sydney • Auckland

First published in 1992 by
Charles Letts an imprint of
New Holland Publishers Ltd

Garfield House
86–88 Edgware Road
London W2 2EA
www.newhollandpublishers.com

80 McKenzie Street
Cape Town 8001
South Africa

14 Aquatic Drive
Frenchs Forest, NSW 2086
Australia

218 Lake Road
Northcote
Auckland
New Zealand

1 3 5 7 9 10 8 6 4 2

ISBN 1 84537 055 4

Printed and bound in Singapore by Tien Wah Press (Pte) Ltd

CONTENTS

INTRODUCTION 7

MATERIALS AND EQUIPMENT 10

BASIC TECHNIQUES 18

GALLERY 24

PROJECTS

TABLE MAT 32

NUMBER PLATE 36

PAVING STONE 40

MIRROR FRAME 48

DRAGON POT 52

FISH BOX 56

TWO BIRDS AT A WATER DISH 62

WATER-FOUNTAIN TABLE 68

FOYER FOOTPRINT 72

INDIAN WATER POT 78

BIRDS AT A FOUNTAIN 82

TERRACOTTA DISH 88

MOSAIC SITES 93

SUPPLIERS 95

INDEX 96

INTRODUCTION

Mosaic is a decorative art form that is achieved by joining together individual units or pieces of stone, glass, etc. to form a unified whole with its own individual identity. The mosaic is dependent on the unit or combinations of units from which it is made, and the way in which the gaps or interstices are designed and planned which separate and unify these units. The unit is known as the tessera, meaning four-cornered or small cube. Tesserae may be made from marble, stone, glass, pebble or a variety of other substances.

The art of mosaic has always played a dual role, being both decorative and functional. Its enormous potential in interior design and architecture as a functional flooring, wall or even ceiling cover has been exploited for centuries.

In some of the earliest-known mosaics found in Ancient Mesopotamia between the Tigris and the Euphrates, now Iraq, in around 3000 BC, tapered clay pegs were pushed into mortar rendering on walls to reinforce the structure. The circular heads of these pegs were coloured and they were arranged in geometric patterns on the rendered surface. In its decorative, aesthetic role, mosaic probably owes much to the ancient art of inlaying found both in Ancient Egypt and Ancient Mexico. Masks and ornaments as well as weapons of war were inlaid or encrusted with mosaic. Various mosaic techniques were developed at that time; the Mexicans, for instance, used turquoise as an

. . . .

The Romans appreciated the great beauty of mosaics, as can be seen in this piece, the Barbarian horseman from Carthage, circa A.D.500 (The British Museum.)

attractive material to apply to the surface of votive or ceremonial objects. Their interest lay in the beauty of the stones and creating a rich textural surface, unlike the Romans who developed more formal methods of shaping and laying the stones (termed 'opus').

The Graeco-Roman times saw great advances in mosaic, initially in a solely functional way as floor or ground coverings, and then, as its decorative potential grew, as wall panels of narrative realism. A more naïve and lively style also emerged, often featured around fountains in gardens, where units of found objects such as shells and stones were introduced.

Floor mosaic proved a durable and practical surface in domestic and public places, much in the way carpets and tiles are used today. The finest examples are of stone and marble cut into tesserae to form highly decorative patterns of great imagination and visual delight. Superbly preserved mosaics are found throughout the countries of the Roman Empire, and they were even incorporated into synagogue floors in Israel. Often *emblemata* were introduced. These were inserted panels of more intricate work, designed to arrest the eye or to act as a central focal point in the overall scheme or theme. It is thought these emblemata were prepared away from the mosaic site in trays or even on hessian and later transferred to their permanent position. Colours in the early mosaics tended to be of natural stone – green, blue, ochre, white, terracotta and black – but gradually highlights of glass were added, probably as early as the second century BC.

The following period, Christian-Byzantine, saw a great flowering of abstract mosaic work. Mosaic art was greatly patronized, and its visual power was used to full effect in major Christian churches such as in Ravenna. (Later the same artists were to decorate the mosques of Jerusalem and Damascus.) This official encouragement inspired an era of technical and artistic experiment. Full use was made of the new material, glass smalti, and a unified system of decoration and hierarchical expression developed. A real understanding of colour emerged. It was discovered that by angling smalti in the mortar, their full reflective quality could be exploited in brilliant plays of light and shadow across the surface. More important still was the realization of the abstract power of form through conceptual imagery as opposed to realism.

A further period of great mosaic activity was in the eleventh and twelfth centuries when the vast decorative schemes of Venice, Greece, Sicily and Rome were created to enhance the Christian religion.

In the fifteenth century the Conquistadors in Central America were using mosaic with great skill to cover ritual objects, employing turquoise and other natural

. . . .

Bowl with Birds and Cat, circa 79 A.D., *Naples Museum. The Romans were keen observers of life, as can be seen in this portrayal of tension between the parrots and the cat.*

stones on wood, stone, shell and even skull bases. Regular, square tesserae were mainly used and the emphasis was on colour and texture rather than imagery. The process used mosaic like a jewelled skin.

Meanwhile, in Europe, during the Italian Renaissance, there was a gradual decline of interest in mosaic as a decorative art form in its own right. Painters used mosaic to create facsimiles of their work, *pitture per l'eternita,* where the fragmentation of the tesserae was so concealed that it was no longer a true mosaic but took on the sheen and semblance of an oil painting, as seen for example in Raphael's *The Transfiguration* in St. Peter's, Rome.

Later, in the eighteenth century, mosaic degenerated into a miniaturist curiosity, where individual smalti tesserae were melted down and drawn into threads of glass known as *smalti filati.* These were used to compose micromosaics with as many as 1,400 tesserae to the square inch. This misplaced expertise showed technical virtuosity but missed the true qualities of mosaic. It was not until the great decorative revival of the Art Nouveau period that mosaic was to be rediscovered and given fresh vigour.

Gustav Klimt, 1862–1918, whose paintings are quasi-pointillist, had a taste for the decorative. He visited Ravenna in 1903 and enthused about the mosaic he saw there. In his murals for the dining room for the Palais Stoclet, Brussels, he incorporated smalti with painting and specially commissed decorative tiles and ceramic shapes.

Antoni Gaudí, 1852–1926, was a pioneer in the decoration of exterior walls with mosaic. He wanted the outer surface of a building to create its own effect. He worked within the Spanish-Moresque tradition by using glazed tiles, and unlike Klimt who had expensive materials made for him, Gaudí used debris and *objets trouvés.* By applying these fragmented materials as a skin around forms, he led the way for three-dimensional work and sculpture to be applied with mosaic.

The inventiveness of Gaudí was to influence the politically conscious Mexican painters and muralists of the 1950s. Using the less expensive vitreous glass, and drawing their imagery from the Pre-Columbian art of the Maya and Teotihuacan cultures, they encrusted public buildings with huge mosaics created in the name of Social Realism. Diego Rivera, D. A. Siqueiros, José Chauvez Morado and Juan O'Gorman headed

*Gustav Klimt, The Kiss, 1905-9.
Preparatory cartoon for a grand frieze
in the Palais Stoclet, Brussels. The
frieze was realized in white marble,
gold smalti and specially made tiles.*

. . . .

this dynamic mosaic force. Once again the essential power of mosaic was used as the visual expression of a strong belief. Islamic art continued to use mosaic as an architect-related art form using pre-shaped coloured ceramic tiles inlaid in a geometric tessellation.

Many twentieth-century artists have used mosaic as their medium: Jeanne Reynal and Joseph Young in America; Hans Unger, Boris Anrep and Eberhard Schulze in Britain; and Jean Bazaine in France. Experiments were done with found objects, and in various forms – sculpture, free-standing mosaic work and projects on a vast scale. Alongside this inventiveness,

however, grew a rather sterile, deadening use of mosaic as a relatively cheap cladding material for the façades of civic and commercial buildings. This misappropriation did much to depopularize mosaic as a true and valid art medium, and this trend was encouraged by many well-known artists who, instead of using mosaic as an expressive medium in its own right, had their paintings translated into durable glass and stone interpretations, or 'pictures for eternity', by expert artisans in the workshops of the Vatican, Ravenna, Spilimbergo and Venice. Marc Chagall, Hans Erni, Oskar Kokoschka, and many others used mosaic in this way.

However, the true spirit of mosaic was kept alive in the mid twentieth-century by Simon Rodia (Watt's Towers, Los Angeles, U.S.A.); Raymon Eduoard Isidore (La Maison Picassiette, Chartres, France); Niki de Saint Phalle (Il Giardino dei Tarocchi, Tuscany, Italy); and Nek Chand (The Rock Garden, Chandigarh, India). Their expressive, naïve inspiration has emerged from an untutored response to mosaic, and all of the artists have experimented with the use of a variety of materials including scrap, glass, china, metal and ceramic in a unique architectural and sculptural way.

Today, many artists are using mosaic as their artistic medium, rejoicing in both its formal qualities and also in its expressive versatility. Artists working in the medium include the following – a selective list that is by no means exhaustive: Lucio Orsoni, Felice Nittolo and Mimmo Paladino in Italy; Jane Muir and Arthur Goodwin in Britain; Claude Rahir in Belgium; Alexandre Korooukhoc in Russia; and Jerry W. Carter and Susan Bacik in the U.S.A.

Mosaic is an appealing medium and mosaic-making is easily adaptable to domestic conditions. There are no special requirements other than a will to explore a natural sense of pattern that is in all of us, combined with a practical approach to working in a relatively slow way. It is time consuming, but can be enjoyed by all. Even the simplest mosaics often have great appeal.

The techniques described in the following pages can be applied to the decoration of ordinary objects or in the creation of works of great size and profundity. The projects illustrated are demonstrated stage-by-stage to encourage the reader to create rather than imitate, and to inspire you to explore the enormous potential of mosaic as a medium for personal expression.

MATERIALS AND EQUIPMENT

MATERIALS

THE MATERIALS used in mosaic-making may be traditional or unique. Listed below are the materials used in the projects in this book; additional materials can include pebbles, shells, stones, marble, slate and any number of found objects. The mosaic artist will unceasingly acquire or procure any tool or object that will facilitate in the making of mosaics. Try, when using a material, to bring out its inherent potential and to be sure that its colour, form or texture is integral to the mosaic as a whole.

SMALTO (I)

The classic mosaic material. Smalti are small, generally opaque glass tesserae, with a cut surface of great reflective power. Glass is coloured when molten with metallic oxides, then the smalti are hand-cut from larger 'pancakes'. Sizes vary but 10 × 15mm (⅜ × ½in) is most commonly used. Smalto is generally classified and sold by colour groupings: golds; reds, oranges and yellows; whites, greens and blues; and blacks, greys and browns.

Smalto antico is a grainier glass, which has extra sand added during manufacture. It looks similar to the type of glass used in the Ravenna mosaics. Just over 1kg covers 30sq.cm (3lb cover 12sq.in).

GOLD SMALTO (I)

Made of silver and gold leaf (24 carat), hammered very thin and put on a coloured glass backing and then covered further with a thin film of glass – again often coloured. The metal is therefore embedded, and can be used in the reverse with the metal shining through the coloured glass. It is hand-cut to various sizes, most surfaces commonly 20 × 20mm (¾ × ¾in).

VITREOUS TESSERAE

Manufactured glass squares of uniform sizes and shapes. Molten glass is poured into waffle-shaped trays and pressed to give a flat upper surface. The underside is bevelled and has grooves which aid good adhesion. The bevelled edge allows the material to curve naturally on three-dimensional pieces of work and makes for a good 'fit' at edges. Often bought in sheets pasted face down on to paper or net, they can easily be removed for sorting. There is a good colour range including a sparkling copperized glass. Vitreous is virtually indestructable and is both frost- and light-proof. The most commonly used size is 20 × 20mm (¾ × ¾in); just under 1kg covers 30sq.cm (2lb cover 1sq.ft).

CERAMIC TESSERAE

These are available glazed and unglazed in an ever-growing selection of colours and sizes. They constitute the cheapest range of bought material. The colour range represents the more natural colours of nature: ochres, greens, terracotta and black and white. They are also particularly good for edging mosaic panels.

MIRROR TILES

Mirror tiles have canvas backings to secure against scratching and weathering. They can be cut with care using mosaic nippers.

A range of materials can be used for mosaic-making – from the classic smalti, to household china and ceramic tiles. In addition to these, pebbles, stones, shells and other found objects can also prove to be excellent surfaces

. . . .

CERAMIC TILES AND HOUSEHOLD CHINA

These create lively textured surfaces for direct working into cement. Both materials can be cut using mosaic nippers. Colours and surface finishes are limitless and large areas of wall can be covered at very little expense, and often at some speed

BASES

The base material for a mosaic is determined by its position – whether internal or external – its size, and the type of tesserae used. Plywood, whether marine or external or ordinary, is suitable for all internal direct working. For general use a thickness of 6mm (½in) is adequate. The projects in this book demonstrate work on net, fired ceramic ware, rendered, second-hand furniture, and wood. Tesserae may also be applied to resin and perspex (plexiglass) bases, both being light and weather-resistant.

ADHESIVES

The type of adhesive used in a mosaic is often determined by the siting of the finished piece and the conditions in which it is made.

CEMENT: an indispensable material with excellent adhesive properties used for bedding, setting and grouting all types of mosaic including glass, marble and ceramic.

E.V.A. (ETHYLENE/POLYVINYL ACETATE): a universal and excellent adhesive and bonding agent.

EPOXY RESIN: a contact adhesive in two components, one the resin and the other the hardener, that have to be mixed before use. It holds well in all conditions, has great strength, weather resistance and lightness. It is,

Tessarae can be stored in glass jars or clear polythene bags for easy identification.

. . . .

however, expensive and needs to be used quickly and in a well-ventilated area.

GUM: a water-based adhesive. Ideal for use in indirect methods where the glass or ceramic tesserae are only to be held temporarily. Easily removed with water.

CEMENT

Portland cement, so called for its colour resemblance to Portland stone, is used throughout the projects in this book. Cement is cheap, responsive, has excellent adhesive qualities and a good neutral colour. Store in a dry location, in a plastic dustbin or similar container. It is alkaline, and so it is advisable to wear rubber gloves when handling.

SANDS

These come in a variety of colours (red, yellow and silver) and grain sizes. Apart from the Paving Stone project (page 40), fine sharp sand of different colours is used throughout this book. If in doubt about the grain size, use a sieve. Coarse sands add greater strength to the mortar, but for small-scale mosaics and grouting, finely sieved sand is invariably used.

CEMENT DYES

The colour range of cement dye is good, and includes green, red, yellow, blue and black. Experiment with these dyes, adding the colour a teaspoon at a time to the dry cement or sand mix, as the colour is permanent and intense. Avoid using white grout unless for deliberate affect, as white tends visually to bleed the colour away from the surrounding tesserae. You will find that the natural grey colour of the cement by its very neutrality tends to enhance the brilliance of the tesserae it surrounds. Containers for cement dyes must be clearly labelled and stored in a safe place.

TOOLS AND EQUIPMENT

SKETCH BOOK: have one of these with you at all times for sketching, note-taking and general scribblings.

PENS, MARKERS AND PENCILS: for making the designs and transferring them to board or base.

BRUSHES: a selection of brushes, including fine artist's brushes, toothbrushes, nail brushes, decorator's brushes and masonry brushes.

RULE OR STRAIGHT EDGE: for designing, measuring and creating borders.

PALETTE KNIVES: for applying adhesive and smoothing mortar.

AWL OR GIMLET: used for boring into wood to position screws or mirror plates before hanging.

GOGGLES, AND NOSE AND MOUTH FILTER MASKS: to be worn whenever working in dusty atmospheres or where there is risk of flying glass particles, etc.

RUBBER/ERASER: for use in drawing.

COMPASSES: used in the execution of curving designs and for measuring.

TWEEZERS: invaluable for 'pricking out', prodding, and moving small pieces around.

SCREWDRIVER: for fixing and hanging mosaics.

PETROLEUM JELLY: for greasing wooden frames and to facilitate removal of concrete slabs.

SCISSORS AND CUTTING KNIFE: for cutting paper and net, for scoring, and for cutting papered mosaic segments in the indirect method.

MOSAIC NIPPERS AND HAMMER AND HARDIE: the tools of mosaic cutting (see page 18).

GRAPH PAPER, TRACING PAPER, PAPER BOARD, AND NETTING: used in design-making (see page 19).

STRONG BROWN PAPER, NETTING, AND WOODEN BOARD: used as bases for mosaic-making.

WOODEN FRAME: for containing concrete slabs. A wooden frame can be made simply at home using strips of 1cm (½in) wood of between 5–7.5cm (2–3in) width. The corners can be mitred or simply 'T'-shaped

together. The length should not be greater than about 50cm (20in) or the concrete slab it contains will become too heavy to handle.

HYDROCHLORIC ACID: an acid which effectively removes excess cement residue (mortar or patio cleansers can be substituted). Containers must be labelled clearly and stored in a safe place.

SIEVE: for sieving fine sand.

BOWL: for mixing cement mortar, and grout.

GLOVES: both surgical (tight-fitting) and stronger rubber gloves to protect hands when working with cement, acid, etc.

CLOTHS AND SPONGES: used for dampening and for cleaning and polishing.

NOTCHED FLOAT: more commonly known as a serrated float, this is used in laying cement beds for floors, and for levelling and rendering walls. Its flat surface is used for giving a smooth surface, and the serrated edge is used to create grooves to form a key for better adhesion.

SQUEEGEE: used in grouting to distribute cement mortar evenly across the surface of the mosaic.

TROWELS: of many sizes and shapes for mixing and applying cement mortar.

BRUSHES: for acid cleaning, polishing and painting.

KNIVES: use to clean off excess cement after direct application of tesserae into cement.

JUG: for holding and pouring water.

THE STUDIO

Mosaicists always expand to fit a space! However, the essentials for working are the following:

Table, workbench or *easel* at a good height for working whether sitting or standing.

Good light in both daylight and at night.

Access to water.

An outside area, if possible, where messy work like grouting and cleaning can be done.

Durable and easily scrubbed and brushed *floor covering.*

Shelves for storing tesserae and materials, etc.

Glass jars and *clear polythene bags* for storage and to ensure quick and easy identification of materials.

Space for storing grouting materials and boards.

A *'clean' area* for drawing and designing.

A *portable trolley* is very useful for holding objects and tesserae for immediate use – as it can be moved to wherever work is taking place.

STUDIO TOOLS AND EQUIPMENT

SKETCH BOOK

PENS, MARKERS AND PENCILS

BRUSHES

GUM, RESIN AND E.V.A.
ADHESIVES

PICTURE HOOKS

RULE OR
STRAIGHT EDGE

CUTTING
BLADES

PETROLEUM JELLY

MOSAIC NIPPERS

SCISSORS

CUTTING KNIFE

HAMMER
AND HARDIE

AWL OR GIMLET

PALETTE KNIVES

GOGGLES,
AND NOSE
AND MOUTH
FILTER MASKS

RUBBER/ERASER

COMPASSES

TWEEZERS AND
IMPLEMENTS FOR
'PRICKING OUT' AND PRODDING

TRACING PAPER

SCREWDRIVER

WOODEN BOARD

GRAPH PAPER

PAPER

TRONG BROWN
APER

TTING

GROUTING AND OTHER EQUIPMENT

HYDROCHLORIC ACID

WATER JUG

CERAMIC TILES
AND HOUSEHOLD
CHINA

WOODEN FRAME

PETROLEUM JELLY

CEMENT

NOTCHED FLOAT

SQUEEGEE

KNIVES

GLOVES

BOWL

CLOTHS AND
SPONGES

SIEVE

SAND

TROWELS

BRUSHES

PRODDER

BASIC TECHNIQUES

CUTTING AND SHAPING

THE HAMMER AND HARDIE

Most cutting is done indoors and creates constant 'puffs' of dust or glass particles. It is advisable, from the start, to learn to cut away from directly under the nose and to one side so that breathing in the dust created by each cut is reduced. If in any doubt wear a simple nose and mouth dust shield. Similarly, when cutting tesserae, if there is a possibility of flying fragments of glass, wear a comfortable pair of goggles. This is an essential tool for cutting marble and smalti. The hammer is curved on one edge and generally has tungsten carbide tips for strength and durability. The weight of each individual hammer is important in enabling tireless and comfortable cutting – it should usually weigh around 1.5kg (4lb). The straight edges of the hammer aim to come into direct contact with the anvil-like edge of the hardie. The hardie, slightly curved and often edged with tungsten carbide, is embedded into an upright log. Place it at a comfortable sitting or standing height so that movement is not restricted when cutting.

The hammer's blow should be light, firm, true and aimed directly above the cutting edge of the hardie, with the tessera positioned at the required angle and held between the thumb and finger, on either side of the chisel edge. Do not despair if tesserae shatter from time to time: cutting is an acquired skill and with practice will become almost second nature. The rewards of perseverance are extreme accuracy in cutting all forms of materials and irregular shapes, and, contrary to what you may initially think, great speed.

MOSAIC NIPPERS

These are made from toughened steel with tungsten-tipped cutting edges, and are suitable for cutting vitreous glass and ceramic tesserae. The legs or handles of the nippers are held as near the end as possible, so that the effort is taken up by the spring. The mosaic tessera should be placed just between the cutting edges with the viewed side uppermost; the cutting edges should be on the line that is to be fractured. By squeezing the legs of the nippers together and exerting equal pressure with the opposite thumb and finger, the tessera will be fractured exactly as wanted.

● To cut in half: hold the nippers open with the cutting edges just holding the tessera halfway along its side.

*Holding the tessera on the
hardie between the thumb and finger,
hit it firmly with the hammer.*

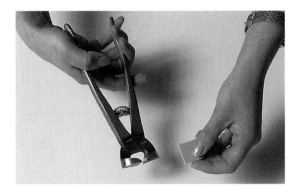

*Place the tessera between the
nippers and squeeze.*

Squeeze the legs together while exerting equal pressure with your thumb and finger holding the tessera. The tessera will cut in half.

● To make quarters: take one of the halves, hold as before halfway along the unbevelled side (if vitreous glass is used), and squeeze with equal and opposite pressure as before.

● To taper a tessera for following a curved form, take a halved tessera and point the cutting edge of the nippers at the desired angle. Squeeze.

● Sixths or eighths are often used for a 'drawing line' in mosaic. First cut the tessera in half and then cut each of these halves into three or four equal parts.

● To cut circles or petal shapes, a slightly different

*Using nippers, tesserae can be
tapered for curved forms.*

technique is used. Hold the idea of the shape in mind (or draw with a marker directly on to the tessera), cut off the four corners, then 'nibble' with the nippers from the outer edge until the required shape is reached. With practice great accuracy can be achieved.

DESIGNING A MOSAIC

A diagram or drawing for a mosaic design has no set rules but calls for simplification and stylization whether it is a copy, or taken from nature or the imagination. Important considerations are:– the site of the proposed mosaic, its proportions, the light source, and environmental colours. Never forget that the material used for mosaic-making is a hard cube of colour – the tessera – which has its own intrinsic properties.

Never let the drawing dominate the mosaic once the drawing is transferred – let the mosaic piece by piece create its own momentum through movement, colour and texture.

Draw to size wherever possible or relevant. This helps gauge the size of the tesserae which are to be used. It also helps, in the initial stages of learning, to draw in or indicate the movement of the tesserae, especially where decisions about direction have to be made. Unless you are using repeating patterns or working within a more rigid framework, draw freehand; this will enhance the effect of liveliness and unpredictability in the design.

Experiment. Use the accidental. Explore through spontaneity and the imagination. Cement these together with a disciplined control and understanding.

METHODS OF
MAKING MOSAIC

There are two basic methods: in the first, each piece is seen as it is cut and placed, but in the second it is viewed only indirectly. These are called the direct method, and the indirect or reverse method.

DIRECT METHOD

This is the most natural and satisfying of mosaic methods. Tesserae are cut and placed directly, face up, on to a base, be it cement, wood, net or ceramic. Drawings or designs can be transferred freehand or, more exactly, by tracing or 'pricking out'. Tesserae may be placed at an angle to increase the power of light reflected from their cut surfaces. Great play can be made of varying the level and the texture of the surfaces, such as matt against shiny.

The direct method is mostly used for murals, hung panels, sculpture, mosaics on three-dimensional surfaces, and in any situation where the surface may not be smooth or level.

INDIRECT OR REVERSE METHOD

When a uniform surface is needed, as in a floor, or when a smooth or weatherproof mosaic is required, for instance in a pool or on a paving stone, or when very large murals are made away from site, the indirect method is invaluable.

The tesserae are cut and stuck *face down* on to strong paper using a water-based glue. The mosaic is only revealed when it is transferred into a cement bed and the backing paper washed off. Because the mosaic is laid flat, the face is smooth and the reflective quality is minimal; interest may be emphasized instead in strong decorative form or through the *andamento* (this term is used to describe the directional movement made by the lines of tesserae, and is often called the flow of coursing of the material).

PRICKING OUT

This is a method of transferring a design on to a freshly rendered wall. The rendering must be at its 'setting' stage, i.e. when it appears to have hardened but is in fact only at an early stage of curing. (After the transferring of the design, it must be covered up with damp cloths or polythene; this allows the evaporation to take place slowly in order to reach its maximum strength.) Fix the paper with the design on (drawn to size) in position on the wall or concrete base (thin metal pins can do this, helped by the clinging nature of the moisture of the mortar). Begin pricking out at the top of the design: using a thin sharply pointed tool, prick the design through the paper and into the soft concrete rendering at intervals of about 1 to 2cm (½ to ¾in). When the whole design has been pricked through, remove the paper. In some cases it may be helpful to join up the small holes made in the cement – use acrylic paint and a brush for this, as it will enable a better 'reading' of the design.

OPUS: LAYING THE TESSERAE

When a tessera is cut and laid, it has an integrity of its own, and certain decisions have then to be made regarding the next piece – one piece leads on to the next and influences it. Certain ways of laying have developed over the years, known as opus. By understanding these traditional methods, contemporary mosaicists gain a deeper understanding of the formal properties inherent in an individual tessera and can influence more control and understanding over the way tesserae are used.

OPUS TESSELLATUM

These tesserae are cut in cube-shaped pieces, sometimes larger than those used in the image, and are placed in horizontal or vertical lines to form a regular fill-in or background pattern around the image. Much used in early Roman mosaics, it is often used to stabilize an image.

OPUS VERMICULATUM

Here tesserae of varied shapes are used to outline an image or main decorative detailing by following the contour lines in a 'worm-like' fashion (see page 66).

OPUS MUSIVUM

A continuation of Opus Vermiculatum, but applied all over the mosaic surface, including any imagery, to give a lively sense of movement throughout (see page 71).

INTERSTICES

The crevices or gaps formed between the placings of mosaic tesserae; the way these are filled and their widths and lengths play an important part in the finished design of the mosaic.

ANDAMENTO

The flow or direction of the tesserae, or 'coursing', often emphasized by the interstices.

MAKING CEMENT AND MORTAR

Cement and mortar are terms that are used synonymously, together or separately. A mortar is made

*Add water to the dry
ingredients and mix well.*

from cement, sand and water (often with the additions of colouring, lime, plasticizers and bonding agents). A concrete is created when an aggregate of small stones or coarser sand is added for increased strength. Each mosaic artist has a favourite 'recipe'. The tried-and-tested mix that has been used throughout the projects in this book is: three parts (cups, or heaped trowels) of sand to one part cement. For greater bonding, or where there is a little uncertainty about this, add E.V.A. adhesive to the water in a ratio of 3:1 (three volumes of water to one equal volume of E.V.A.).

The ingredients must be thoroughly mixed together in a dry state, on a board if larger quantities are used, or in a bowl for smaller quantities, using a trowel or hands protected by rubber gloves. Heap into a mountain shape and form a crater in the centre.

Using a trowel, mix from the centre out by slowly adding water or water plus E.V.A. The mortar should always be firm. If it is runny its bonding properties are weakened and cracking may occur in the drying-out.

Never hurry the drying-out process; this is a chemical reaction which occurs as soon as water is added. The mixture dries by curing, the slower the better; allow three or four days for this, and keep covered with polythene sheets or damp cloths, towels or newspapers throughout.

SLURRY

An essential part of the procedure, ensuring a good bonding with an existing wall or floor. When the mortar is prepared, put a small quantity in a dish and add more water (or water and E.V.A.). Mix together with the trowel or palette knife to form a thickish slurry. Use a soft absorbent brush, and, after wetting down the area (wall or floor), apply a generous coating of the slurry, before trowelling on the cement mortar. Many old mosaics have come 'unstuck' because this small but essential part of the procedure was not adhered to.

GROUTING

Except when using smalti, most mosaics will need grouting when completed. This is a method of rubbing cement mortar into the surface of the mosaic to fill the interstices or crevices. It strengthens the mosaic by tightly securing the tesserae. More importantly it draws attention to the spaces between the mosaic tesserae and emphasizes the design's movement or flow. It is a very pleasing and essential part of mosaic-making.

To make the grouting, the ratio of sand to cement is 3 or 4:1. Cement colour may be added to the dry mixture at this point to emphasize the *andamento* or to harmonize or contrast with the colour palette of tesserae used. Water is added to make a fairly dry mix, which is pressed or trowelled into the crevices with gentle but firm pressure. Protect your hands with gloves or use the squeegee to do this.

*Spread the grout over the
mosaic with a trowel.*

*Press the grout into the crevices
with your hands.*

*A squeegee can also be used to
press in the grout.*

Cement does not adhere to wood unless the wood has been initially coated with E.V.A. However, E.V.A. may be added to the water in the grout mixing, at a ratio of three volumes of water to one of E.V.A., to ensure a bond. If the grouting takes place over a cement-based mosaic, wet the area thoroughly before pressing the grout into the crevices.

Clean away excess grout with cloths or brushes. Leave covered under damp cloths, newspaper or polythene to cure for about three days.

Grouting may seem tedious, but it has the exciting quality of unifying the mosaic.

CLEANING MOSAICS

If no cement is involved in the mosaic process, e.g. through the use of tile cement or other bedding adhesives, brushing or polishing the finished mosaic with cloths may be all that is needed to give a clean finished surface. When cement is used, the most effective cleaner is hydrochloric acid, a powerful substance which eats away cement.

When the mosaic is finished and grouted, a cement scum will appear on its surface when dry. Pour a little of the acid into a plastic or glass container, and dilute it with at least 15 times the amount of water. Undiluted hydrochloric acid has a vicious bleaching action, so observe all safety precautions and wear gloves throughout the procedure. Any spillage or splashing should be immediately washed with great amounts of water. Ideally the cleaning process is best done out of doors.

Carefully brush the diluted hydrochloric acid over the mosaic; a 'fizzing' action will occur. Directly the area has been brushed with the acid, wash clear with copious amounts of clean water as any remaining acid could continue eating into the mosaic. Allow to dry naturally, then polish with soft cloths, or if china, brush with a masonry brush. The mosaic is now clean and brilliant. Should any marks occur at a later date on its surface, use water and detergent to remove.

*Clean away any excess grout
with a cloth or a brush.*

FRAMING MOSAICS

This applies in the main to panels hung as pictures and to the finished edges of murals. Furniture often has a 'lip' to work into. Work may be edged with framing tiles (see page 78 or 82), or with proprietary fillers, and sanded smooth when dry. Wooden frames with mitred corners often frame a mosaic adequately. Cut or uncut mosaic tesserae may themselves be used to frame a work (see pages 48 and 62), and often a painted edge suffices.

FIXING MOSAICS

Mosaic may be fixed as a permanent feature or hung as a picture for easy removal. The methods for fixing vary depending on the materials used and the siting of the mosaic.

*Screw the eyes into the wood,
and hang with picture wire.*

*Screw the plates into the back
of the mosaic where required.*

MIRROR PLATES

Use for any mosaic on wood that needs a vertical placing, such as a plaque, mirror, or larger mural on a board that needs secure fixing. The plates can be used on the sides or fixed from the top and bottom. Screw into the wood at the back of the mosaic, taking care to use screws shorter than the thickness of the board. Finally, after marking and drilling the holes and using plugs, screw the plates to the wall.

SCREW EYES

Use where the mosaic is portable and is to be hung as a picture. The length of the screw eye must be shorter than the thickness of the wood. Mark the two corresponding spots in the back where the screw eyes are to go. Use a gimlet or awl to bore into the wood base, then screw the eyes tightly into the wood. Use picture wire to join the two screws – double-thickness usually suffices. Hang, using double picture hooks.

PERMANENT FIXING

For permanent placing of a mosaic on a board. Drill holes and countersink before starting on any mosaic work. Taking care not to cover the holes, complete the mosaic work including the grouting. (A countersink is a tool used to bevel the edge of a hole, so that when the screw/nail is in position the head of the screw is on a level with the surface and does not stand proud of it.) Mark the position of the mosaic on the wall through the drilled holes with a pencil or pointed tool. Remove, drill holes into the wall, and sink in rawlplugs. Screw through the mosaic to the wall until secure. Cut tesserae and fix over the screw heads to hide their whereabouts, then grout and clean the small areas.

GALLERY

THESE EXAMPLES OF the work of Elaine M. Goodwin, Eve Jennings and Glen Morgan demonstrate a wide range of decorative mosaic work, and reflect a diverse use of materials and techniques, as well as the artists' creative use of pattern and colour.

All of these mosaics are, of course, individual to the artists themselves, but they will also inspire you to make your own experiments whether you are seeking to create a purely decorative feature or a piece that is practical as well.

~

Flowers in a Black and Gold Vase
GLEN MORGAN
60 × 45cm (24 × 18in)
This is a strongly coloured vitreous glass flower piece of ornate symmetry, with a liberal use of gold smalti in the design and framing border to make a richly glowing mosaic surface.

Horizontal Bird Tree

ELAINE M. GOODWIN

122 × 61cm (48 × 24in)

A mosaic work incorporating vitreous glass, ceramic and smalti. The piece was created to complement a small Haiku poem:
'Pigeon breast colours smudge the sky
Birds gather darkening the dusk.'

. . . .

Yellow Tulip

GLEN MORGAN

25 × 25cm (10 × 10in)

Glen Morgan uses mosaic to express her sense of the ornate, delighting in richly textured surfaces alive with colour and movement.

This yellow tulip mosaic was produced by the direct method, using ceramic and vitreous glass. Indebted to Art Nouveau in its stylization, its strong linear form is ideally suited for translation into mosaic. The mosaic tile was made as one of a series of ornate tiles used to decorate a bathroom wall.

. . . .

Dragon

GLEN MORGAN

66 × 84cm (26 × 33in)
Based on a traditional dragon design, this large wall-mounted mosaic makes full use of different mosaic materials: glass and gold to give a strongly coloured image, ceramic for a contrasting matt background, and single orange-red vitreous glass tesserae as the flames.

. . . .

Terracotta Lizard

ELAINE M. GOODWIN

40 × 40cm (16 × 16in)
This small panel, of smalti, vitreous glass and ceramic, forms a backdrop in a sunny kitchen behind a collection of terracotta utensils. It adds a lively note to the kitchen and evokes a Mediterranean feel.

. . . .

Dodo

ELAINE M. GOODWIN

86 × 86cm (34 × 34in)
This work was designed as part of a bestiary series for a child's play area. It was made directly on to plywood using many types of mosaic material, including vitreous glass, smalti and ceramic.

. . . .

Peacock Box

GLEN MORGAN

18 × 26 × 13cm (7 × 10 × 5in)
A treasure chest to hold trinkets and jewellery, made by applying tesserae – vitreous glass, mirror and gold smalti – directly on to a simple and cheaply bought wooden box, transforming it into an ornate object of beauty and colour rather in the manner of Ancient Mexican mosaics, where semi-precious stones and glass were applied to objects to form a richly textured skin.

. . . .

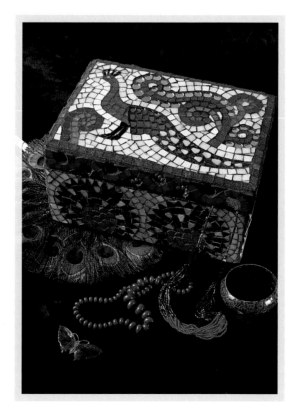

Poppy

EVE JENNINGS

30 × 25cm (12 × 10in)
This is the second in a small series of flower pieces using vitreous glass and the direct method. Eve's interest in studying flowers is apparent, and the scarlet poppy mosaic is a direct interpretation of some stunning garden blooms.

. . . .

Rinascita

ELAINE M. GOODWIN

152 × 100cm (60 × 40in)
A large wall-hung mosaic designed for a sitting area in a home. Various opera are used for special effects – notice particularly Opus Palladianum, more commonly known as crazy paving, in the background. This gives a highly intricate and interesting surround to the strong image of the tree. Gold, smalti, vitreous glass, shell, mirror and ceramic were all used.

. . . .

Big Bird Tree

ELAINE M. GOODWIN
184 × 92cm (72 × 36in)
Elaine M. Goodwin has been working with mosaics for over fifteen years, producing pieces both for exhibition and for public and private commission. She regards her personal work as 'visual Haiku' or 'stone poems', which frequently include the image of the tree.

This mosaic work incorporates vitreous glass and gold smalti. The mosaic was done after returning from working in India and evokes for the artist the colours and more formal arrangement of imagery found in Indian miniatures. The eyes in the top corners are a symbolic ward against evil; the conservatory where this is hung therefore has a guardian in the form of a tree.

. . . .

Iris

EVE JENNINGS
30 × 25cm (12 × 10in)
This is a picture for the home. The rich border incorporating varying shades of blue vitreous glass intensifies the strong decorative nature of the mosaic.

. . . .

Five Bird Tree

ELAINE M. GOODWIN

76 × 76cm (30 × 30in)

A decorative fire screen made with vitreous glass in the direct method. The screen acts as a colourful focus for the room in the summer; in winter the mosaic is removed when fires fill the grate. It is temporarily fixed at the edges by an easily removed filler.

. . . .

Paving Stone

EVE JENNINGS

36 × 36cm (14 × 14in)

Eve Jennings has a strong sense of structure and understanding of the formal properties of the mosaic tessera, resulting in mosaic work that is strong in pattern and that has an underlying feel for order, balance and harmony.

This vitreous glass mosaic is one of a series of concrete-based mosaics for placing in a herb garden. They can be stood on when gathering herbs for cooking, and add colour in winter.

. . . .

TABLE MAT

E V E   J E N N I N G S

A SIMPLE YET striking project with a practical function, produced by the direct method. The terracotta, black and white colouring is in direct line of descent from the Graeco-Roman tradition, where white marble, black basalt and terracotta stones or pebbles were used to make bold and geometric floor coverings.

A number of variations could be made up on this theme using a simple palette, and cut and uncut tesserae arranged in different geometric formats. A series of finished mosaics would make a particularly attractive set of place mats.

Size: 30cm (12in) square

MATERIALS AND EQUIPMENT

● *mosaic tesserae: vitreous –
see colour palette in project* ●
*plywood: 6mm (¼in) or
9mm (⅜in) thick, 30cm
(12in) square* ● *mosaic
nippers* ● *E.V.A. adhesive* ●
palette knife ● *scoring knife* ●
tweezers or similar implement
● *graph paper* ● *pencil* ●
ruler ● *black wood dye and
brush* ● *rubber gloves* ● *red
sand* ● *cement* ● *bowl* ●
cloths ● *trowel* ● *hydrochloric
acid and brush*
· · · · · ·

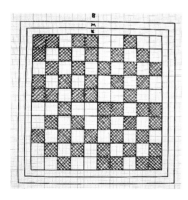

1 Draw the required design on a
sheet of graph paper.

2 Transfer the drawing to the
board allowing for a little space
between the tesserae. (The main
design occupies a 21cm (8¼in)
square.)

3 Score the board with a sharply
pointed cutting knife, to give a
key for the adhesive.

4 Using the palette knife, apply
the adhesive to the reverse side of
the black and white tesserae, i.e. the
grooved side. The process is often
referred to as 'buttering' the
tesserae.

5 Apply the 'buttered' black and white tesserae to the board to form the chequered mosaic square. The border can now be started.

6 Continue to apply the border.

7 Surround the chequered board with terracotta tesserae cut in half (see page 19). Follow with a line of halved white tesserae. Finally surround the whole with a line of black, uncut tesserae to make a framing border.

Leave the mosaic 24 hours to dry thoroughly. (The E.V.A. adhesive will dry from white to colourless.) The mosaic is now ready for grouting (see page 21). When the grouting has been left to cure and dry for three to four days, put on rubber gloves and clean off the surface cement with hydrochloric acid. Rinse clean with copious amounts of water and allow to dry naturally. Polish with a soft cloth, then paint the outer edges with the black wood dye. The mosaic is now ready for use.

NUMBER PLATE

E V E   J E N N I N G S

USING THE MOTIF of a circle within a square, a simple yet bold number plate is created which can easily be recognized and read from a street position. More complex examples based on this direct method of application and fixing can be made for name plates, work places and signs.

Size: 12mm (½in) thick, 20cm (8in) square

MATERIALS AND EQUIPMENT

● *mosaic tesserae: vitreous — see colour palette in project (plus alternatives)* ● *exterior or marine plywood: 12mm (½in) thick; 20cm (8in) square* ● *mosaic nippers* ● *silicon waterproofer and brush* ● *epoxy resin adhesive* ● *spatula* ● *scoring knife* ● *tweezers or similar implement* ● *pencil* ● *tracing paper* ● *compasses* ● *4 screws and 10 rawlplugs* ● *rubber gloves* ● *cement* ● *fine sand* ● *bowl* ● *cloths and sponges* ● *hydrochloric acid and brush*
. . . . . .

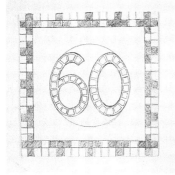

1 Drill and countersink four holes near the corners of the board for the screws that will fit the mosaic to the wall. Draw the design on paper.

2 Using tracing paper, transfer the design to the board. Score the board.

3 Cut the light and dark blue tesserae into quarters (see page 19) and fix with adhesive to the border. Leave gaps large enough to take quarter tesserae over the screw holes. Cut extra dark blue tesserae and taper where necessary for the curve of the number (see page 19) and outline the number.

4 Complete the border surround and numbers with two rows of light blue tesserae, and begin to fill in the numbers.

5 Use larger pieces to fill the inner corners of the square in a third blue colour. Continue filling in. Leave to harden for 24 hours, then grout the mosaic (see page 21) and, when dry, acid–clean (see page 22). Position the mosaic on the outside wall and drill four corresponding holes; then, using rawlplugs, screw on to the wall. When the mosaic is secured in position, seal the edges by covering the cut ends of the wood with a waterproof sealant, smooth and clean. Place four quarters of tesserae over the screw heads and stick into position. Grout and clean these small areas so that the method of fixing is entirely hidden from view.

PAVING STONE

E V E   J E N N I N G S

PRODUCED BY THE indirect method, this paving stone of a bright camomile herb can be placed outside in a small formal herb garden. The formation of circles in a square complements the desire for peace and quiet order and the colours were chosen to harmonize rather than compete with nature. This could be one of a series depicting different herbs and plants.

Size: 30cm (12in) square

~

MATERIALS AND EQUIPMENT

● *mosaic tesserae: vitreous –*
see colour palette in project ●
mosaic nippers ● *brown paper*
● *tracing paper* ● *gum*
(water-based) ● *brushes* ●
toothbrush ● *pencil* ● *ruler*
● *compasses* ● *rubber/eraser*
● *tweezers or similar*
implement ● *wooden frame:*
31cm (12½in) square ●
supporting board: a little
larger than the frame ●
wooden baton: over 31cm
(12½in) long ● *petroleum*
jelly ● *reinforcing wire and*
wire cutters ● *trowel* ● *dish* ●
sand: fine and coarse ● *cement*
● *rubber gloves* ● *squeegee* ●
bowls and container ●
hydrochloric acid and brush ●
cloths, sponges and newspaper
. . . . . .

1 Draw the design to size on paper.

2 Trace off the design and transfer to the brown paper: it is important that the drawing is laid down in reverse, i.e. mirror image, on the brown paper.

3 Cut a mixture of tesserae in halves and then divide each half into three for the stems of the flowers (see page 19).

4 Using the gum, lay the green tesserae pieces smooth (top)-side down on to the brown paper. Cut into halves and taper the white tesserae to make the flower petals (see page 19).

5 Cut yellow ellipses from halved tesserae for the flower centres. When the flowers are completed, fill in the inner circle with quarters of the off-white tesserae wherever possible. Encircle with mid-green then quartered white tesserae followed by halved dark green glass.

The framing square border is of whole dark green tesserae, with the corner triangles outlined in white halved pieces and infilled with mid-green large pieces. (Refer to these corners in the design (see page 42). Four different versions of how to resolve corner designs are given: a, b, c, d. Each solution gives a different look to the mosaic as a whole.)

Leave the finished mosaic to dry thoroughly.

6 You will need a supporting board the same size as the papered mosaic. Grease the inner sides of the frame with petroleum jelly. Then, transfer the mosaic on its paper to the board and place the greased frame over the top.

7 Sprinkle a thin layer of fine dry sand over the mosaic, taking care to cover all the crevices but not so much that it covers up the tesserae.

8 Use brush to distribute the sand evenly.

9 In a bowl or container mix the coarser sand with the cement to make a stiffish mortar and half fill the frame.

10 Cut the reinforcing wire to the size of the interior frame and place over the first layer of mortar, making sure the wire does not touch the wooden frame or buckle upwards above the height of it. Put the remainder of the mortar on top of the wire and fill to the top of the frame.

11 The surface can now be trowelled smooth, taking care that the corners are sufficiently compacted. Level with the wooden baton.

Leave under damp newspaper or damp cloths covered with a polythene sheet for four days for the cement to cure. The cement must not be left to dry out too quickly as this will weaken the strength of the concrete.

12 Gently ease the mosaic slab out of the wooden frame and turn over. Moisten the brown paper with wet cloths and peel off the brown paper taking great care that the mosaic tesserae do not become dislodged. The mosaic is now revealed. Brush away any sand lodged in the interstices with the toothbrush. Make a small quantity of grout (see page 21) and grout the surface of the mosaic. Leave to cure for two days, then acid-clean in the normal way (see page 22). The paving stone is now ready for placing in any exterior position in the garden or patio, as it is completely weatherproof.

MIRROR FRAME

GLEN MORGAN

THIS FREE-FLOWING design is based on circles and spirals which allow the mosaic to grow naturally from the initial placings of the tesserae. It is created by using the direct method. The vitreous tesserae used are those in the copper vein range, and their intermittent sparkle emphasizes the reflective surface of the mirror without detracting from the functional nature of the mosaic.

Size: 60 × 45cm (24 × 18in)

MATERIALS AND EQUIPMENT

● *mosaic tesserae: ceramic and vitreous – see colour palette in project* ● *mirror tiles* ● *mosaic nippers* ● *mirror cut to size (do not cut until frame is made)* ● *paper* ● *pencil and marker pen* ● *wood glue* ● *E.V.A. adhesive* ● *scoring knife* ● *spatula* ● *palette knife* ● *rubber gloves* ● *grey sand cement* ● *trowel* ● *cloths and sponges* ● *bowl* ● *hydrochloric acid and brush* ● *plywood: 12mm (½in) thick; 60 × 45cm (24 × 18in) for base and 2 strips 60 × 9cm (24 × 3½in) for sides, and 2 strips 27 × 9cm (11 × 3½in) for top and bottom of frame.* ● *mirror plates and screws*
● ● ● ● ● ●

1 Draw the design to size on paper.

2 Make a simple frame, using the plywood for both the base and frame. Glue the frame to the base with a wood glue and clamp or hold it in position with heavy weights for 24 hours. Transfer the design to the wooden frame by drawing freehand (to keep the forms loose). Score both the frame and the base with a sharp cutting knife.

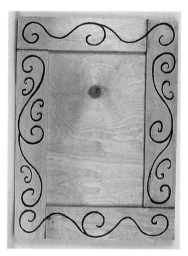

3 Begin by cutting tesserae for the main lines of the arabesque pattern in a dominant colour in vitreous glass. Cut mirror tiles into circles (see page 19) and incorporate them into the design.

4 Continue using three further colours in vitreous glass to add to the main lines and spirals. When the border mosaic is completed, glue the mirror to the base using the E.V.A. adhesive.

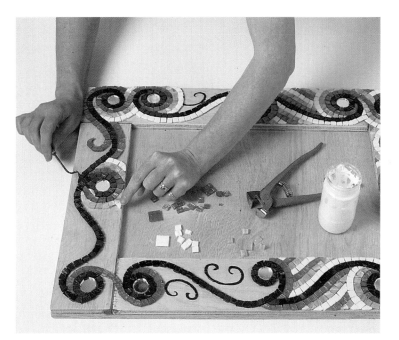

5 Cut ceramic tesserae to fit in the area between the surface of the mirror and the surface of the mosaic, and glue these to the sides to make a neat edging for the mosaic and to secure the mirror in position.

Glue uncut ceramic tesserae to the outer edges of the wood to frame the mosaic. Grout in the normal way (page 21) using fine sand, and acid-clean (see page 22).

The mosaic may now be fixed to a wall using mirror plates attached either to the sides or at the top and bottom. In this way the mirror is lined up vertically with the wall.

DRAGON POT

GLEN MORGAN

CONTINUING THE TRADITION of dragon designs on planters, this earthy variation, produced using the direct method, adds an extra dimension and colour to an otherwise standard terracotta garden pot. The image of the dragon is left in relief on the pot, its rich palette of colour set against the natural terracotta colour of the base.

Choose either a pot with a glazed interior, or waterproof the inside of the pot with a coating of silicon waterproofer if it is to be used filled with earth. This helps to prevent dampness seeping through and weakening the adhesion of the tesserae. The use of an epoxy resin adhesive similarly ensures against dampness.

Size: approx. 25cm (10in) in diameter

~

MATERIALS AND EQUIPMENT

● *terracotta-coloured clay pot:*
25cm (10in) diameter ●
mosaic tesserae: vitreous and
gold smalti – see colour palette
in project ● *mosaic nippers* ●
marker pen and pencil ●
paper ● *epoxy resin adhesive*
● *dish or tile for mixing* ●
spatula ● *waterproofer*
(silicon-based), optional ●
brush ● *tweezers or similar*
implement ● *cement* ● *red*
sand ● *trowel* ● *gloves* ●
cloths and sponges ● *bowl* ●
hydrochloric acid and brush
· · · · · ·

1 Draw the design to size on paper.

2 Transfer the design (freehand) to the pot.

3 Mix together the two components of the epoxy adhesive in a dish or on a tile. Cut the scale shapes and glue to the main body of the dragon using the occasional gold scale to enliven the surface.

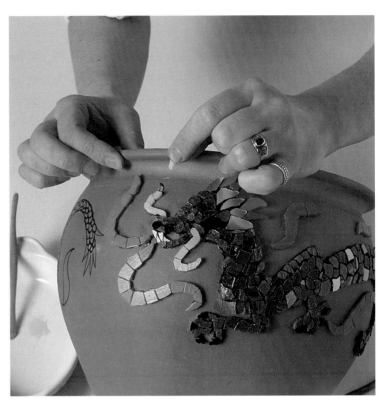

4 Cut the main head features –
eyes, nostrils, etc. – and fix to
the pot.

5 Complete the dragon body and
flames. Do not fill in any of the
background as the design is to be
left standing proud of the terracotta
background.

Repeat the process with the
second dragon on the reverse side
of the pot.

6 Wearing rubber gloves, grout
the mosaic area, taking extra care
around the edges (see page 21).
Acid-clean (see page 22), fill the pot
with compost and plant a flower!

FISH BOX

GLEN MORGAN

IN THIS MOSAIC, produced by the direct method, the arabesque forms are representational of waves – an apt and integral part of the marine design. In using mixed media that incorporate gold and mirror tiles, a rich, textural and sparkling quality is achieved. The three-dimensional form of the box with its many facets provides a challenge to the mosaicist to find solutions for joining edges and corners while keeping the design free and fluid.

Size: 28 × 17 × 17cm (11 × 6¾ × 6¾in)

~

MATERIALS AND EQUIPMENT

● *basic wooden box with hinged lid: 28 × 17 × 17cm (11 × 6¾ × 6¾in)* ● *mosaic tesserae: vitreous, ceramic gold, and mirror – see colour palette in project* ● *mosaic nippers* ● *marker pen* ● *pencil* ● *paper* ● *E.V.A. adhesive* ● *palette knife* ● *scoring knife* ● *tweezers or similar implement* ● *grey sand* ● *cement* ● *rubber gloves* ● *trowel* ● *cloths and sponges* ● *bowl* ● *hydrochloric acid and brush*

. . . . . .

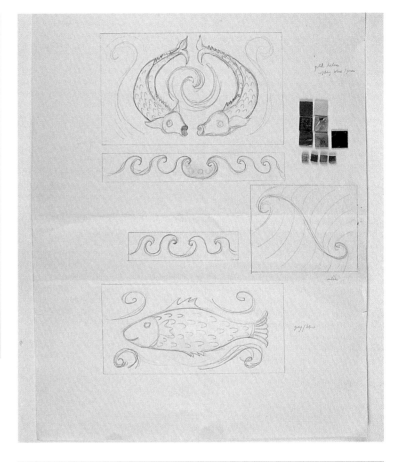

1 Draw the design for the lid top and all four sides of the box to size on to paper, using a repeated design on corresponding sides and a unique design on the lid.

2 Transfer the design to the box freehand. Score all the surfaces of the box.

3 Cut the scale shapes for the two larger fish and glue them on to the longer sides of the box. Begin work for the lid in a similar way, but use gold smalti as a dominant colour.

4 Complete the fish on the longer
sides and completely surround
with a white line of tesserae. Begin
then to work on the wave forms;
take great care to co-ordinate the lid
pattern to the main body of the
box.

Complete filling in the tesserae as
shown in the finished photograph.

5 On the two smaller sides, begin
the abstract wave forms,
incorporating the mirror tesserae.

6 Complete the filling in of the side design.

7 Use the bevelled edge of the white mosaic tesserae at all the edges to give a neat appearance and clean edge. Complete the lid.

Grout in the normal way, taking especial care at all corners (see page 21). Acid-clean (see page 22) to finish.

Two Birds
At a Water Dish

ELAINE M. GOODWIN

THIS PRACTICAL YET unusual mosaic is produced using the direct method, and the colours can be varied to suit individual schemes. Birds at a water dish is a traditional theme for mosaicists. The Romans were fascinated by the theme, as were the Byzantine Christians. As a contemporary theme for a wash-hand basin splash back, it continues to be appropriate. The birds are taken from sketches of birds drawn while working on mosaic murals in India. The mosaic contains mixed tesserae in a restrained palette of black, white and gold.

Size: approx. 55 × 35cm (22 × 14in)

~

MATERIALS AND EQUIPMENT

● *mosaic tesserae: ceramic, vitreous and gold smalti – see colour palette in the project* ● *mosaic nippers* ● *marker pen* ● *close-weave fibre netting: 65 × 45cm (25 × 18in)* ● *paper* ● *silicon-backed paper* ● *E.V.A. adhesive* ● *scissors* ● *tweezers or similar implement* ● *palette knife* ● *rubber gloves* ● *sponges and cloths* ● *knife* ● *cement* ● *fine sand* ● *large bowl* ● *trowel* ● *strong tile or wood block for tamping down* ● *hydrochloric acid and brush*
. . . . . .

1 Draw the design to size on paper. Cover the design with the netting, allowing the design to show through, and then draw over the design with a marker on to the net, simplifying the shapes and lines if necessary. Remove the paper from underneath the net and replace with silicon-treated paper (this stops the adhesive from sticking to the working surface).

2 Cut ceramic and black, white and gold smalti into quarters and frame the drawing with a bold edging. This will also help keep the net flat and secure for working on.

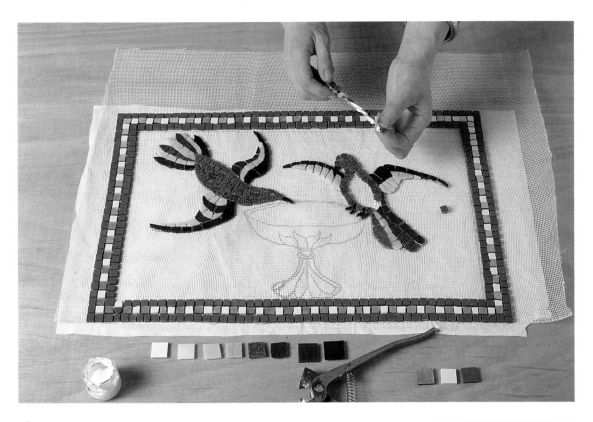

3 Use the vitreous glass in shades of black and grey to fill in the birds, using simple shapes to emphasize their form and feathers.

4 Use the gold and vitreous tesserae to build up the water dish. Complete, using the white vitreous tesserae cut mostly in quarters to outline the form before filling in the background.

5 Fill in the background following the strongest outlines, to give a sense of movement to the design (an Opus Vermiculatum pattern, see page 30). When completed, allow the adhesive to dry thoroughly for at least 24 hours.

6 Cut the net close to the outer edge of the mosaic. The mosaic on the net is now ready for moving and attaching to the bathroom wall.

7 Prepare the area of wall behind the wash-basin by marking it out and coating with diluted E.V.A. adhesive. It may also be necessary to score the wall for better adhesion. Prepare a cement mix, adding E.V.A. to the water for mixing (see page 20). The mortar should not be too wet. Trowel the mortar on to the wall so that it is about 5mm (¼in) thick. (Any excess cement overlapping the area needed for the mosaic can be cleaned off at a later stage.)

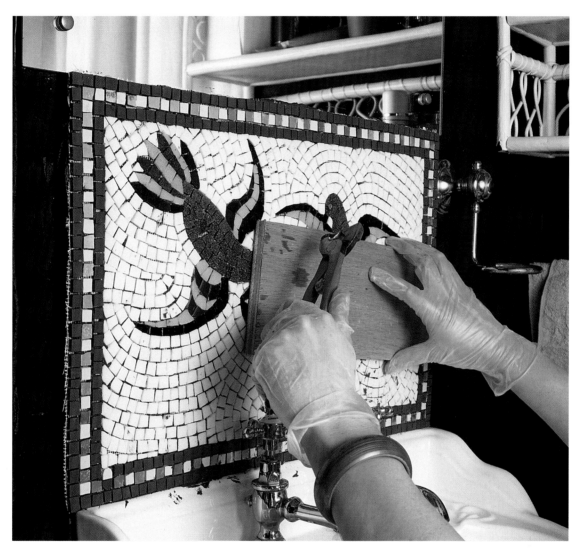

8 Carefully lift the mosaic and place it in position, holding from the top edges. When the position seems correct, tamp★ the mosaic lightly all over using the tile or wood block. The cement should just rise to the surface of the mosaic through the holes in the net. Check for an even surface, using a length of wood as a baton if necessary. Leave for about one hour.

With a knife, gently clean away any excess cement from the sides or surface. Keep the mosaic damp for about three days with wetted sponges or cloths. Then grout the mosaic (see page 21), taking care at the edges to bevel them or add a small mosaic edge.

Acid-clean (see page 22). The mosaic can now be 'wiped over' for cleaning and any splashes will not have a harmful effect on the surface. The mosaic is now a permanent part of the wall.

★ Tamping is an action to embed mosaic firmly. After the mosaic on net or paper is placed in position, cover the area with a block of wood or tile and, using a hammer or the side of the mosaic nippers, gently knock the mosaic to its correct depth.

WATER-FOUNTAIN TABLE

ELAINE M. GOODWIN

THE ART OF MOSAIC gives new life to this otherwise unremarkable table. A design of a water fountain was adapted to fit the circular form of the table by using an octagonal frame within the circle, reminiscent of a Moghul pool or an Islamic low gaming table. The restrained palette is offset by gold smalti used both for their bright gold sparkle and for their luminescent backing glass. The simplicity of the mosaic's colour and design, created using the direct method, is its great strength.

Size: 56cm (22in) diameter

~

MATERIALS AND EQUIPMENT

● *a wooden table: 56 cm (22in) diameter (any table may be used which is sturdy and has a surface that can be made smooth and clean.)* ● *mosaic tesserae: vitreous, ceramic, and gold smalti – see colour palette in the project* ● *mosaic nippers* ● *E.V.A. adhesive* ● *palette knife* ● *scoring knife* ● *tweezers or similar implement* ● *sandpaper* ● *brush, paint and wax for table legs* ● *tracing paper* ● *pencil* ● *marker pen* ● *rubber gloves* ● *cement* ● *green cement colour pigment* ● *fine sand* ● *trowel* ● *squeegee* ● *hydrochloric acid and brush* ● *cloths and sponges* ● *bowl*
. . . . . .

1 The surface of the table should be clean, and sanded smooth and level, ready to accept the mosaic.

2 Draw the design to size on paper. Be sure that the design is sympathetic to the shape of the surface of the table and its overall form. Transfer the design by tracing on to the table. A symmetrical design will shorten this process. Score the table.

3 Begin by cutting the black, grey, gold and green glass into quarters; mitre the tesserae as they join at each of the eight corners. (To mitre is to join pieces of mosaic tesserae together at the edges to form a 45° angle. Cut tesserae at an angle of 45°.)

4 Turn the gold smalti over to reveal the brilliant blue–green backing glass and cut into sixths (see page 19). 'Draw' the water lines with these.

5 Cut the black tesserae into sixths and outline the fountain base, then begin to fill this in following the most dominant lines of the image.

6 Begin the background in white ceramic tesserae by following both the lines of the solid imagery and the water. Continue in a natural progression outwards. This gives emphasis to the 'arched' forms of the water and also great fluid movement to the whole mosaic.

When completed, grout the surface of the table, adding a small quantity of green cement colour pigment to the dry grout to make a sharper contrast between the tesserae and the interstices (see page 21). Pay particular attention while grouting to the edges of the table; in some cases the table may have a natural 'lip', as here, which will automatically frame the mosaic.

Acid-clean (see page 22).

Lightly sand the legs of the table and apply paint; in this case the colour is the same as that of the grout. Rub wax into the legs and polish to a dull shine with soft cloths. The table is now ready for use and can withstand normal everyday use; take care however that the gold smalti are not scratched.

71

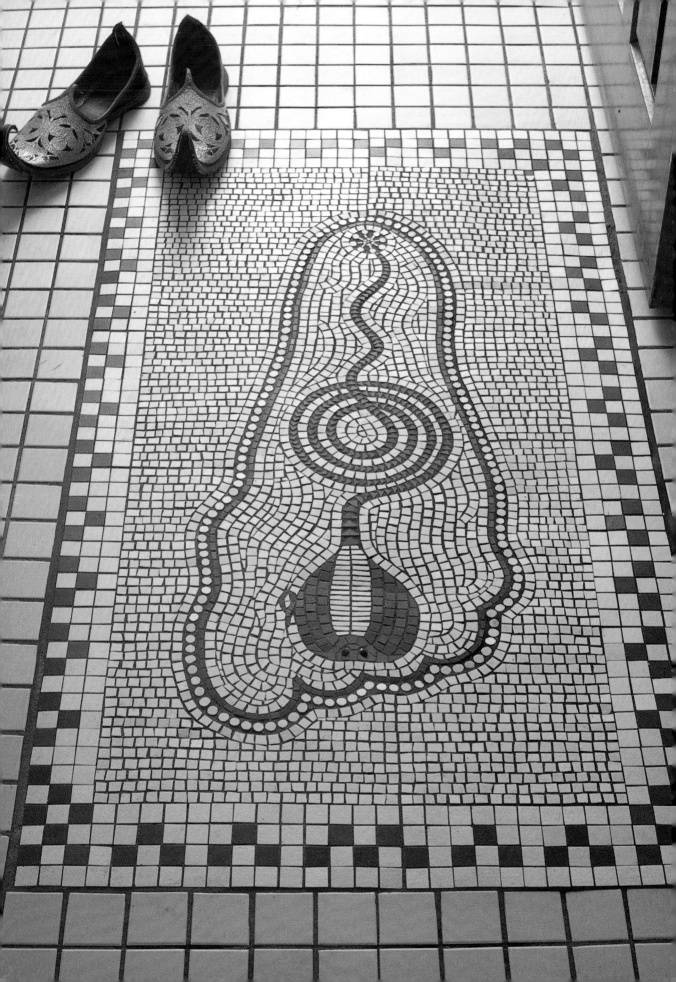

FOYER FOOTPRINT

ELAINE M. GOODWIN

THE FOOTPRINT, according to Indian tradition, is as auspicious an image as is the hand motif. The cobra with raised hood signifies energy, also inherent in the red colour used. Thus the imagery in this small entrance foyer mosaic guards and protects the household.

This *emblema* was produced using the indirect method, and was 'let-in' to an area left by surrounding tiles laid on concrete. This is in the much-practised tradition of the *emblema* of Roman times.

The functional nature of mosaic when used as a floor covering is unsurpassed; it is practical, extremely hard-wearing and easily maintained.

Size: 108 × 61cm (42 × 24in)

~

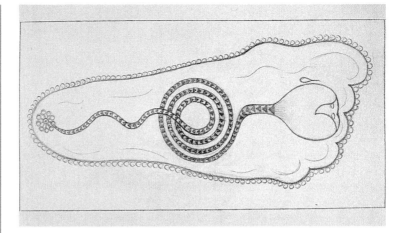

MATERIALS AND EQUIPMENT

● *mosaic tesserae: ceramic – see colour palette in the project* ● *mosaic nippers* ● *strong brown paper: minimum 112 × 71cm (44 × 28in)* ● *any water-based glue or gum* ● *small brush* ● *tracing paper* ● *pencil* ● *marker pen* ● *sharp cutting knife* ● *tweezers or similar implement* ● *palette knife* ● *ruler* ● *rubber gloves* ● *cement* ● *sand* ● *dish and brush* ● *notched float* ● *trowel* ● *wooden block for tamping: 30cm (12in) square* ● *cloths and towels* ● *hydrochloric acid and brush* ● *bowls and buckets* ● *spirit level* ● *hammer*
. . . . . .

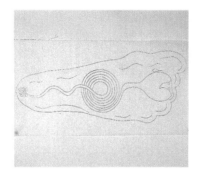

1 Draw the design to size on paper.

2 Trace the design with a soft pencil, reducing the line to its essentials and simplifying any intricacies.

3 Turn the tracing paper over, put into a central position on the brown paper, and draw over the design. The drawing on the brown paper should now be in reverse, i.e. a mirror image, to the original.

Cut the ceramic black tesserae into eighths (in half and divide each half into four) and outline the main image with these by glueing the good (top) surface to the brown paper. Put just enough glue on the brush to secure the piece temporarily to the brown paper, but not so much as to make the brown paper crinkle up. Surround this form with circles (see page 19) cut from quarters, remembering always to glue the good (top) surface directly on to the paper.

Cut triangles in terracotta tesserae (quarters cut on the diagonal), and use these to delineate the snake form.

4 Fill in the centre part of the snake spiral with ceramic white quarters: this also acts as a 'good' edge for the form.

5 Mark in some of the contours of the footprint with white ceramic, to give added interest and movement to the design.

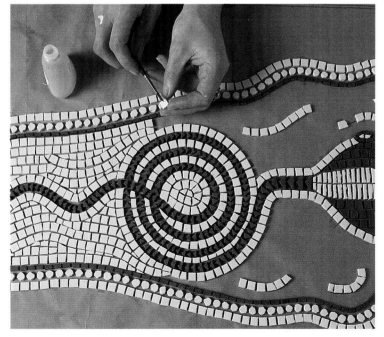

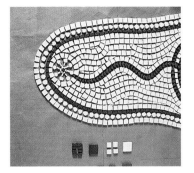

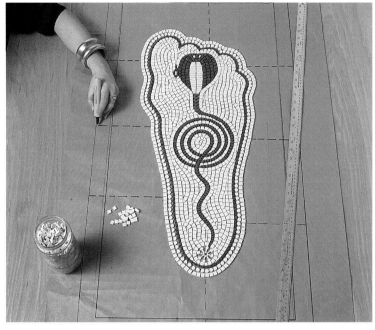

6 Outline the snake with a single line of white tesserae and continue to fill in the inner area of the foot.

7 When completed, use a marker pen to draw in the cutting lines, i.e. the lines which will be cut with a sharp knife to divide up the mosaic into manageable segments for fixing to the floor.

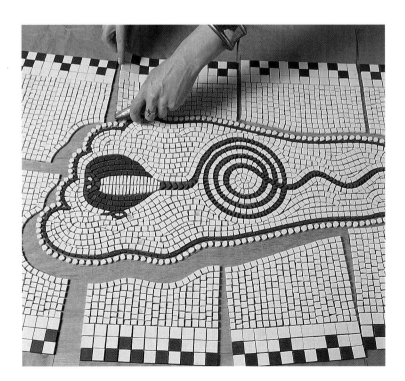

8 Use square black and white ceramic for the border, and position in. Cut white ceramic quarters to fill in the background. Allow to dry before cutting into movable segments and transfer on to a flat board.

At the site where the mosaic is to be fixed, check that the floor has a concrete base before beginning to lay the paper mosaic.

Mix up a quantity of cement (see page 20), enough to cover the whole area with a thickness of about 6mm (¼in) or at least just under the height of the surrounding floor tiles. Wet the floor where the *emblema* is to be embedded. Put a little of the cement mortar in a dish and water down to form a slurry, then brush over the entire area. (E.V.A. adhesive may be added to the water if there is any uncertainty of the mosaic bonding to the existing floor surface.)

9 Assemble at site the hammer, spirit level, wood block, notched float and trowel, together with the mosaic on a board. It may help to number the papered back of the mosaic sections for easier assemblage.

Trowel the cement mortar over the entire area, using the notched float to spread an even surface. Starting at the 'toe' end, carefully lift the corresponding mosaic section and, using your eye and a steady hand, align the papered mosaic into position before carefully laying it. (This is a method potentially full of minor problems, and it is a good idea to enlist a willing helper to assist with the placing of the mosaic.) There is very little leeway in positioning the mosaic for fear of dragging off the small tesserae, so be sure and certain in all the placings.

When all the subsequent sections are in position, use the wood block and hammer to tamp the mosaic gently into its bed so that it rests on a level with the surrounding floor tiles. Any uncertainties can be adjusted using the spirit level.

When satisfied that the whole mosaic is level, leave the area covered with damp cloths or towels for about four hours or until the cement appears to have set enough to clean the edges using a knife. After 24 hours gently peel off the brown paper, taking care not to dislodge any of the tesserae. This is an exciting process as the surface of the mosaic is revealed for the first time.

Should any pieces have moved out of alignment, use the tweezers to remove them, clean the small area of old cement and replace the tesserae in position with a small quantity of fresh cement to which E.V.A. has been added in the mixing. This small corrective procedure can be left until the end of the peeling process. Remember, a little natural error can humanize the whole design.

When satisfied that the mosaic is true, cover the area again with damp cloths for a further three days until the curing process is complete. Make up sufficient grout (see page 21) to cover and fill the crevices of the whole *emblema* and wipe clean. When 'cured', acid-clean (see page 22).

The mosaic is now part of a permanent floor surface and can be treated as such, i.e. walked on.

INDIAN WATER POT

ELAINE M. GOODWIN

THE CHATTI OR Indian water pot is seen all over India standing in doorways or in a draught keeping water cool. In this design it is combined with a lizard. Together, the pot and lizard form a decorative wall panel evoking the everyday essence of Indian life and the juxtaposition of time through the fleeting behaviour of the lizard.

The wall panel, which is created using the direct method, uses ceramic in a minimal way and smalti in particular. The delight of smalti is their irregular and reflective surface and their intensity of colour. This small panel gives a hint of the possibilities of the material and its beauty. The project also demonstrates the use of the hammer and hardie, which has been used for cutting marble and smalti for over 2,000 years.

Size: 46cm (18in) square

MATERIALS AND EQUIPMENT

● *mosaic tesserae: ceramic, smalti and gold smalti – see colour palette in the project* ● *plywood: 12mm (½in) thick, 45cm (18in) square* ● *hammer and hardie (for smalti)* ● *mosaic nippers (for ceramic)* ● *E.V.A. adhesive and tile cement (if mosaic is to be left ungrouted)* ● *pencil* ● *marker pen* ● *knife for scoring* ● *palette knife* ● *tweezers or similar implement* ● *2 screw eyes* ● *wire* ● *brush* ● *grouting material (sand, cement, water bowl, rags, rubber gloves, hydrochloric acid, brush), optional*

Note

Traditionally smalti were left ungrouted. When tile cement is used, the smalti are pressed into it, allowing just enough cement to rise up the sides of the tesserae and to semi-grout them. In this way the full beauty of the material can be appreciated while its irregular surface is held secure by the tile cement. If the mosaic is grouted, E.V.A. adhesive should be used in the normal manner. The grouting will somewhat diminish the intensity of the colour, but on a small-scale piece, the work is 'pulled together' by the grout. The choice is yours.

· · · · · ·

1 Draw the design directly on to the board, being aware of how the design will 'sit' in relation to the space surrounding it and the edges of the board.

2 Using the black ceramic tesserae, outline the image of the water pot.

3 Using the black smalti cut into thirds with the hammer and hardie (see page 18), outline the lizard form. Again using the hammer and hardie, cut very small tesserae in the blue and gold smalti. Fill in the lizard form using a chequered design of alternate colours.

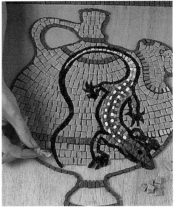

cement and brush to polish the surface of the tesserae. (The ceramic border may be grouted and cleaned independently, by using masking tape to segregate this area from the rest.) Hang as a picture using screw eyes and wire fixed in the back of the wood base.

4 Outline various contours of the water pot with gold smalti.

5 With the pale terracotta-coloured smalti, cut mainly into halves, follow the contours of the water-pot shape.

Using the ceramic black, make a simple border surround – the regularity of the border will heighten the textural quality of the irregular smalti. Then, using the white smalti cut into halves, fill in the background using Opus Tessellatum – one line surrounding the form followed by continuous horizontal lines from edge to edge.

Finally frame the mosaic panel with further ceramic tiles. If using E.V.A. adhesive, grout (see page 21) and acid-clean (see page 22). If tile cement has been used, use a stiff brush to clear away any excess

BIRDS AT A FOUNTAIN

ELAINE M. GOODWIN
EVE JENNINGS AND
GLEN MORGAN

THIS MOSAIC WAS a small group project. Many mosaics throughout history are unsigned as they are the outcome of group participation and a certain anonymity prevails. In large-scale projects of some duration, a joint identity or group consciousness emerges when translating the design on to a wall.

This mural was made by the direct method, and entirely with second-hand china that was either broken or chipped. The uneven surface of the broken china, like expensive smalti, reflects the shifting outdoor light and creates a richly sparkling surface.

Size: 135 × 105cm (54 × 42in)

~

MATERIALS AND EQUIPMENT

second-hand china: ceramic and tiles, sorted into colours • *discarded mirror fragments* • *mosaic nippers* • *paper: 135 × 105cm (54 × 42in)* • *marker pen* • *ruler* • *sharp-pointed tool* • *dish and brush* • *sieve* • *bowls and buckets* • *trowels* • *board for cement-mixing* • *rubber gloves* • *knives* • *polythene sheeting for covering the mosaic* • *masonry brush* • *hydrochloric acid and brush* • *cloths* • *red sand* • *cement* • *masonry paint and brush, optional*

Note

The mosaic is applied to a brick wall freshly rendered with sand and cement. The 'pricking out' technique is done a few hours after rendering when the mortar appears to have set. The area should be kept damp for about three days after this to allow the cement to 'cure' naturally before mosaic work begins on it.

. . . . . .

1 Draw the design to size on a large sheet of paper. Allow extra space for framing tiles if required.

2 A few hours after the wall is rendered, transfer the design to the wall by the 'pricking out' process (see page 20). When the rendered wall is 'cured', work can begin.

3 In general, and wherever applicable, work from the top of the wall or design downwards – this not only prevents the cement from dropping on to previously worked areas but also lessens the risk of washing tesserae off during the wetting of freshly completed areas.

Early on in the mural, begin to frame the allotted area with a tile border. Cut the corners at 45° for a neater fit. Framing helps to retain the work and give a good 'set' edge to work to when it comes to doing the background.

Wearing rubber gloves throughout, mix a quantity of cement (see page 21) for about one hour's work at a time and keep near at hand. Put a little of this cement mortar in a dish and add extra water to make a slurry. Brush generously over a small area for one bird after having thoroughly soaked the area first. (The cement applied to the wall covers up the pricked-out drawing line; use a knife to re-draw in the cement by aligning its form and position to the existing uncovered area.) Cut each china tessera as needed and piece by piece build the bird's form, positioning each tessera and using the mosaic nippers to tap the piece 'home' gently but firmly (hitting with the sprung mosaic nipper in this way creates just enough force to secure it in the cement bed).

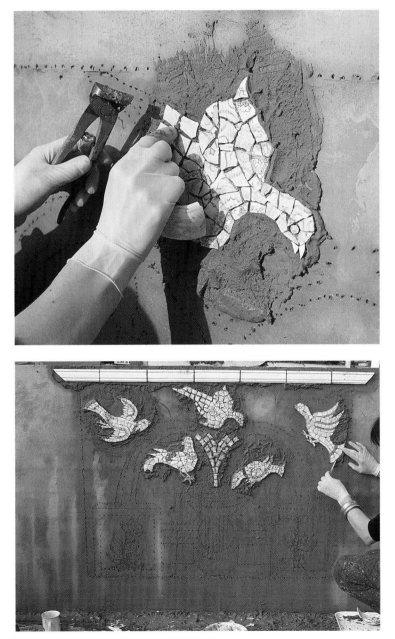

4 Continue to build each bird in the same way. Re-wet the wall each time before applying the slurry and cement, and make small fresh mixes of mortar as needed.

At the end of a day's session, clean the areas around the mosaic with a knife, cutting away the mortar as close as possible to the tesserae; this ensures a closer bonding between one day's work and another. Also, clean away with a knife any excess cement that has risen up above the individual tesserae. Always cover the mosaic with heavy-duty polythene sheeting between sessions; this helps moisture retention within the cement and slows down evaporation, thus creating a stronger mortar.

5 Before continuing, always wet the mosaic all over with copious amounts of water. Complete the fountain, keeping in mind the colour of the background, which should enhance and contrast with any imagery used. In this design lighter coloured china was used for the birds and the fountain, and darker, richer china was reserved for the background.

The two flower tubs provide a good opportunity to add strong colour notes to the design and incorporate some highly decorated crockery.

When the main images of the mosaic are completed, work on the background can begin. This is an immensely exciting procedure as the image changes as it becomes surrounded by colour and texture. It often happens that a colour 'runs out'. This forces a change of plan and leads to interesting variants. Working in this direct way requires more spontaneity and quick decision-making than studio or work-space creations. Being aware of this encourages a freer state of mind and results in lively design and greater enjoyment of the whole corporate experience.

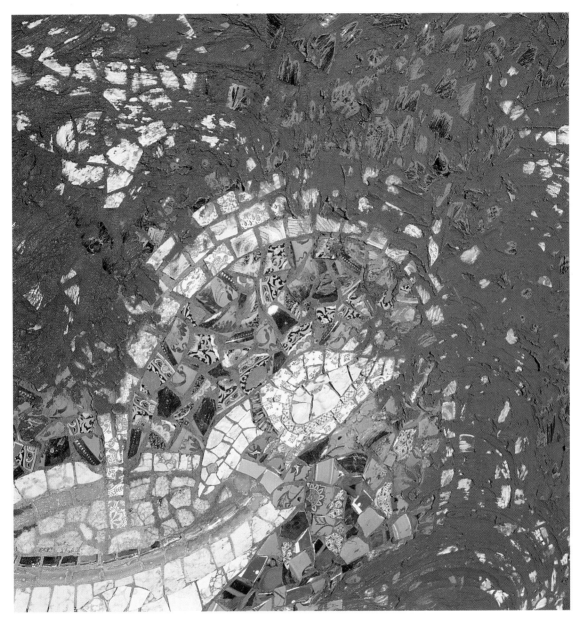

7 When the last pieces have been put in, make a large quantity of stiffish grout (see page 21) and, wearing heavy-duty gloves, rub it into all the crevices, taking care over the rough and uneven surfaces. This is a slower job than often imagined and working as a group is an added advantage.

After the grout has dried, acid-clean (see page 22), and polish using the mortar brush. If required, paint the surrounding wall and clean or re-tile the area in front of the mural. Celebrate the completion.

TERRACOTTA DISH

GLEN MORGAN

A SIMPLE TERRACOTTA dish is the base for this mosaic, which is made using the direct method. The thistle image, taken directly from nature, is simplified into decorative components for the design – the circle and diamond. Many plants can be used in this way and their petals, leaves and flower stems turned into strong decorative features, such as irises, poppies and tulips. The white background gives a striking contrast to the essentially naturalistic colours chosen.

Size: approx. 30cm (12in) diameter

~

TERRACOTTA DISH

MATERIALS AND EQUIPMENT

● terracotta-coloured clay dish: 30cm (12in) diameter ● mosaic nippers ● mosaic tesserae: vitreous – see colour palette in project ● marker pen and pencil ● paper ● E.V.A. adhesive ● palette knife ● tweezers or similar implement ● rubber gloves ● red sand ● cement ● trowel ● gloves ● cloths and sponges ● bowl ● hydrochloric acid and brush

. . . . . .

1 Draw the design to size on paper.

2 Transfer the design (freehand) to the dish.

3 Cut circles (see page 19) for the main shapes of the thistle head and glue these to the base of the dish.

4 Cut diamond shapes and rectangles for the thistle body and stamens and glue these also to the base of the dish.

5 Cut and glue thistle and foliage shapes for the sides of the dish; these are smaller, simplified, versions of the main thistle and foliage shapes on the base of the dish. When gluing the tesserae to the sides of the dish, let the E.V.A. adhesive on them get quite tacky by leaving them exposed to air for about an hour before use, as E.V.A. is initially quite liquid. This prevents the tesserae from slipping down the sides of the dish.

6 Fill in the background, first on the base and then the sides. Leave a neat edge around the top of the dish by placing the uncut bevelled edge of the tesserae uppermost. Grout in the normal way, taking especial care along this upper edge (see page 21). Acid-clean (see page 22), then polish with a soft brush.

MOSAIC SITES

MOSAIC SITES

The following examples are chosen to show the versatility and quality to be found in mosaics worldwide:

AUSTRALIA Melbourne, Metropolitan Fire Brigade.

AUSTRIA Vienna, Secession Building. Decorative mosaic work on the façade and urns. Early twentieth century.

EGYPT Sinai, Monastery of St. Catherine. Apsidal mosaic in fine Late Justinian style. Sixth century.

FRANCE Paris, Louvre. Excellent Roman examples and ancient Sumerian.

GERMANY Frankfurt-am-Main, Dresdner Bank. Elegant and restrained. Heinz Mack, 1980s.

GREECE Thessalonika, Sante Sofia. Superb eighth-century and ninth-century Christian figures.

ISRAEL Jerusalem, The Knesset. Floor fragments depicting the Twelve tribes. Marc Chagall, 1960s.

ITALY Otranto, Cathedral basilica pavements. Lively and naive. Twelfth century.

Ravenna, Parco della Pace. Various contemporary two-dimensional and three-dimensional works.

Sicily, Piazza Armerina. Pavements with strong African influence. Fourth century.

MEXICO Mexico City. Many mural examples of works by Rivera, Eppens, O'Gorman and Siqueiros. 1950s.

PORTUGAL Coimbra. Excellent *in situ* Roman floor mosaics. Third and fourth centuries.

SPAIN Cordoba, Cathedral. Decorative Islamic mosaic work in the Mihrab of the old mosque incorporated into the Cathedral. Tenth century.

SWEDEN Stockholm, The Banqueting Room in the City Hall. Neo-Byzantine style. Einar Forseth, 1950s.

TUNISIA Tunis, The Bardo Museum. Vast and finely preserved collection of Roman mosaics. Third and fourth centuries.

TURKEY Istanbul, Santa Sofia. Many fine Christian fragments. Eleventh to thirteenth centuries.

UNITED STATES New York, Coney Island, Façade of the William O'Grady School. Ben Shahn, 1950s.

MOSAIC IN THE UNITED KINGDOM

BOGNOR REGIS, West Sussex. Superb figure mosaics. Circa 300 AD.

BRADING, Isle of Wight. Fine figure mosaics. Circa 300 AD.

EXETER, Devon, public murals. Multi-themed murals; mixed media, predominantly scrap and recycled. Elaine M. Goodwin and Group 5, 1986 onwards.

GLASGOW, Strathclyde, the Easterhouse mosaic. Sociopolitical landscapes. William Hamilton, George Massey and many others, 1980s.

HULL, Humberside. Various lively mosaics. Circa 300 AD.

LEEDS, Yorkshire, the Romulus and Remus mosaic. Circa 300 AD.

LONDON The Albert Memorial. Mosaic work by Salviati and his workshop. Late nineteenth century.

The British Museum. Various, including the Hinton St. Mary mosaic (circa 350 AD).

The National Gallery. Floor depicting the 'modern' age; indirect method. Boris Anrep, 1927–52.

Tottenham Court Road Underground Station. Mosaics on a musical/mechanical theme. Eduard Paolozzi, 1986.

ST. ALBANS, Hertfordshire, Verulamium. Fine mosaics, including the 'shell' mosaic. Circa 200 AD.

TAUNTON, Somerset, the 'Virgil' mosaic. Circa 300 AD.

SUPPLIERS

Local DIY and hardware stores stock many useful tools and adhesives, and household tiles and small quantities of mosaic tesserae may be found in local tile firms. All the materials and equipment in this book may be obtained from the following firms, most of which will send orders by mail:

UK

EDGAR UDNY & CO LTD,
The Mosaic Centre
314 Balham High Road
London SW17 7AA
United Kingdom
Tel: 020 8767 8181
Fax: 020 8767 7709
(Ceramic tiles, vitreous glass, smalti and gold smalti, mosaic nippers and other mosaic tools)

DW & G HEATH (CROYDEN) LTD,
19 Portley Wood Road,
Whyteleafe,
Surrey CR3 0BQ
United Kingdom
Tel: 020 8657 6349
(Large stockist of mosaic tools and materials: vitreous glass, smalti, glazed and unglazed ceramic tesserae)

REED HARRIS LTD,
Riverside House
27 Carnworth Road
London SW6 3HR
United Kingdom
Tel: 020 7736 7511
(Marble and ceramic tiles)

US

AMERICAN MOSAIC CO,
912 First Street NW
Washington, DC 20001
USA

RAVENNA MOSAIC CO,
3126 Nebraska
St Louis, Missouri 63104
USA

MOSAIC CRAFTS INC,
80 West Street (nr 6th Avenue)
New York, NY 10012
USA

AUSTRALIA

GLASS CRAFT AUSTRALIA,
54-56 Lexton Road
Box Hill North
Victoria
Australia
Tel: 61 3 9897 4188

NEW ZEALAND

TILE WAREHOUSE,
Unit 7A
33 Kaiwharawhara Road
Wellington
New Zealand
Tel: 04 473 9659

INDEX

A

Adhesives, 11
Ancient Egypt, 7
Andamento, 20
Art of mosaic, 7

B

Base materials, 11
Big bird tree, 30
Birds
    at a fountain, 83–87
    at a water dish, 63–67
    horizontal bird tree, 26

C

Cement, 11, 12
    dyes, 12
    making, 20, 21
Central America, 8
Ceramic tesserae, 10
Ceramic tiles, 11
China, use of material, 11, 83
Christian–Byzantine period, 7
Cleaning, 22
Cutting and shaping, 18, 19

D

Decorative art form, mosaic
    as, 8, 9
Designing mosaics, 19
Dodo, 28
Dragon, 27
Dragon pot, 53–55
Dyes, 12

E

Emblemata, 7
Epoxy resin, 11, 12
Equipment, 13–17
Ethylene polyvinyl acetate
    (E.V.A.), 11

F

Fish box, 57–61
Five bird tree, 31
Fixing, 23
Floor mosaic, 7
Flowers in a black and gold
    vase, 24
Foyer footprint, 73–77
Framing, 23

G

Gallery, 25–31
Gaudí, Antoni, 8
Gold smalto, 10
Goodwin, Elaine M, 26–31, 63,
    69, 73, 79, 83
Grouting,
    equipment, 16, 17
    method, 21, 22
Gum, 12

H

Hammer, 18
Hardie, 18
Horizontal bird table, 26

I

Indian water pot, 79–81
Interstices, 20
Iris, 30

J

Jennings, Eve, 29–31, 33, 37,
    41, 83

K

Klimt, Gustav, 8

M

Making mosaic, methods of,
    19, 20
Materials, 10–13
Mesopotamia, 7
Mexico, 7
Micromosaic, 8
Mirror frame, 49–51
Mirror tiles, 10
Morgan, Glen, 24–28, 49, 53,
    57, 83, 89
Mortar, 12
Mosaic nippers, 18, 19

N

Number plate, 37–39

O

Opus, 7, 20
    opus musivum, 20
    opus palladianum, 29
    opus tessellatum, 20
    opus vermiculatum, 20

P

Paving stone, 31, 41–47
Peacock box, 28
Poppy, 29
Portland cement, 12
Pricking out, 20

R

Rinascita, 29

S

Sands, 12
Slurry, 21
Smalto, 10
Studio, requirements for, 13

T

Table mat, 33–35
Table, water-fountain, 69–71
Tamping, 67
Techniques,
    cement and mortar, making,
        20–21
    cleaning, 22
    cutting and shaping, 18, 19
    designing, 19
    fixing, 23
    framing, 23
    grouting, 21, 22
    making mosaic, 19, 20
    opus, 20
    pricking out, 20
Terracotta
    dish, 89–92
    lizard, 27
Tesserae
    buttering, 34
    ceramic, 10
    laying, 21
    meaning, 7
    vitreous, 10
Tools, 13–17
Two birds at a water dish,
    63–67

V

Vitreous tesserae, 10

W

Water-fountain table, 69–71

Y

Yellow Tulip, 26